# GIANCARLO STANTON

Lerner Publications Company
A division of Lerner Publishing Group, Inc.
241 First Avenue North
Minneapolis, MN 55401 USA

For reading levels and more information, look up this title at www.lernerbooks.com.

Main body text set in Albany Std 15/22. Typeface provided by Agfa.


**Library of Congress Cataloging-in-Publication Data**

Names: Fishman, Jon M., author.
Title: Giancarlo Stanton / Jon M. Fishman.
Description: Minneapolis, Minnesota : Lerner Publications, [2018] | Series: Sports
    All-Stars | Includes bibliographical references and index. | Audience: Ages: 7–11. |
    Audience: Grades: 4 to 6.
Identifiers: LCCN 2018007522 (print) | LCCN 2018013286 (ebook) |
    ISBN 9781541524651 (eb pdf) | ISBN 9781541524576 (library binding : alk.
    paper) | ISBN 9781541528031 (paperback : alk. paper)
Subjects: LCSH: Stanton, Giancarlo, 1989—Juvenile literature. | Baseball players—
    United States—Biography—Juvenile literature. | Miami Marlins (Baseball team)—
    History—Juvenile literature.
Classification: LCC GV865.S754 (ebook) | LCC GV865.S754 F57 2018 (print) | DDC
    796.357092 [B]—dc23

LC record available at https://lccn.loc.gov/2018007522


Manufactured in the United States of America
1 - 44533 - 34783 - 5/7/2018

# CONTENTS

# CATCHING
# BABE RUTH

Giancarlo Stanton
runs the bases after
hitting a home run
at Marlins Park in
Miami, Florida.

**The Miami Marlins and Atlanta Braves game on September 28, 2017, wasn't important.** The season was near its end. The Marlins and the Braves both had losing records. Many fans watched just to see if Marlins outfielder Giancarlo Stanton would hit another mighty home run.

Stanton entered the game with 57 home runs. It was the 10th most home runs ever hit in a Major League Baseball (MLB) season. If he could hit two more before the end of the year, he'd tie baseball legend Babe Ruth for ninth most on the list.

Stanton's teammates celebrated with him
after he hit his 59th home run.

Stanton came to bat in the fourth inning. Braves
pitcher Julio Teheran threw the ball. It curved over the
plate and Stanton swung. *Crack!* The ball soared over
the outfield fence for a home run. The blast gave Miami
a 5–0 lead.

He crushed another huge home run in the eighth
inning. The ball rocketed up and over the seats in left

field. Stanton's smash made the final score 7–1. And it tied him with Ruth at ninth on the all-time home run list.

Miami's season ended a few games later. Stanton's 59 home runs made history, but his future lay with a new team. On December 11, 2017, the Marlins traded Stanton to the New York Yankees.

Stanton was introduced as a member of the New York Yankees in 2017.

Stanton stands 6 feet 6 inches (2 m) tall and weighs 245 pounds (111 kg). His teammate Aaron Judge is 6 feet 7 inches (2 m) and 282 pounds (128 kg). Stanton and Judge are two of the biggest MLB players ever.

Panorama City is a neighborhood in Los Angeles.

**Giancarlo Stanton was born on November 8, 1989, in Panorama City, California.** He grew up in a nearby neighborhood called Sunland.

8

Giancarlo *(left)* has a sister, Kyrice *(right),* and a brother, Egidio.

He took to sports right away. A family photo shows Giancarlo playing with a football before he could even walk. When he was three, his parents brought him to a baseball **clinic**. After that, he was hooked on the sport.

Giancarlo was a big, strong kid. And he could crush baseballs. At 11 years old, he could blast the ball up to 250 feet (76 m). He hit a home run in a Little League game that stunned the people watching. The ball sailed over the outfield fence, bounced off a telephone pole, and rolled all the way back to the infield.

Giancarlo was known for being very athletic in high school.

In 2003, Giancarlo began attending Verdugo Hills High School. The next year, coach Angel Espindola joined the school's baseball team. He was shocked by Giancarlo's hitting power. "Since I had just started coaching, I remember seeing him and thinking, 'Is this normal for a high school kid?'" Espindola said. "Obviously, it wasn't."

Giancarlo transferred to Notre Dame High School (NDHS) in 2005. The school has a history of good baseball teams. Former MLB stars such as Jack McDowell attended Notre Dame. Giancarlo played baseball and other sports too. He was a star **wide receiver** for the football team and led the basketball team in scoring.

During his freshman year of high school, Giancarlo (back row, middle) played on the junior varsity baseball team.

Giancarlo had to decide what to do after graduating from high school in 2007. He could go to college. Any college baseball team in the country would have been glad to have him. Schools such as the University

Giancarlo gives some credit for his baseball skills to his father. Mike Stanton often filled a bucket with baseballs and pitched them to his son. Then Giancarlo would think about how to improve his hitting as his father collected the balls.

Former Miami Marlins owner Jeffrey Loria and Stanton talk with the media in 2014.

of Southern California wanted him to play football. Instead, Stanton entered the 2007 MLB **draft**. The Marlins chose him with the 76th overall pick. He had become a **pro** baseball player at the age of 17.

Stanton warms up before games by tossing baseballs with his teammates.

**MLB players get lots of exercise during the season.** Stanton shows up early to the ballpark on game days. He heads to the stadium's gym to stretch and loosen his muscles. Gear such as stretchy bands helps him warm up.

Stanton also warms up for games with batting practice.

Next, Stanton takes swings in the **batting cage**. Someone may toss the ball to him, or he might hit off a **tee**. Other times, he uses a pitching machine. The machine can send a ball zooming as fast as MLB pitchers can throw. Then the team goes to the field for batting practice. Players take turns hitting and fielding balls. Stanton does all this before games even begin.

With 162 games scheduled for each team, MLB seasons can wear down players. To get his body ready,

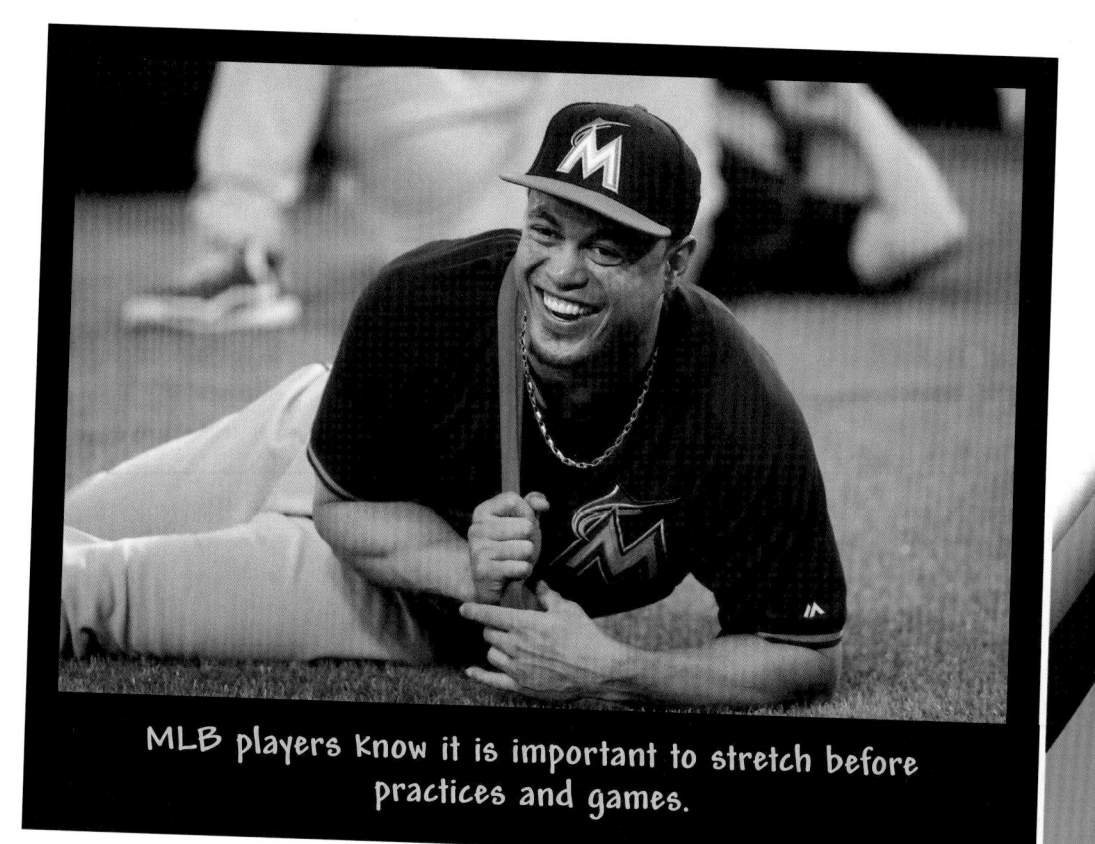

MLB players know it is important to stretch before practices and games.

Stanton returns to California in the **off-season**. Back in his home state, he finds fun ways to work up a sweat.

Stanton spent a lot of time on California's beaches as a kid. As a pro baseball player, he trains on the beach. Stanton sets up a course on a sandy hill. Then he **sprints** up the hill. He may wear a heavy vest to make it more difficult. His feet sink into the sand, forcing him to work even harder. The soft sand also helps prevent injuries.

Push-ups and sit-ups are two of Stanton's favorite exercises. He likes how quickly they help him work up a sweat. He does 100 push-ups and 100 sit-ups in less than five minutes! Lifting heavy weights is also on Stanton's workout schedule.

Have you ever tried yoga? Stanton has done it since high school to help his muscles stretch more easily. Yoga also strengthens his stomach and back muscles.

Stanton (*left*) is known for eating Kit Kat bars in huge bites rather than breaking them up!

In 2018, he shared a video that shows him pushing a cart backward up a steep hill. Two men stand on the cart. Stanton holds a heavy **dumbbell** in each hand. He posted a message with the video: "Work until you've reached your limit. Then . . . set a higher one."

Stanton began a high-**protein** diet in high school. As an adult, he needs even more protein to fuel his active life. He drinks special shakes to get all that he needs. Stanton also eats loads of fruits and vegetables. He loves chocolate for a snack, especially Kit Kat bars.

**Late in 2014, rumors swirled about Stanton.** Baseball reporters said he was about to sign a huge **contract** with the Marlins. Fans were shocked when they finally learned the details.

Stanton enjoys getting dressed up for events.

Stanton had agreed to a 13-year contract that would pay him $325 million. It was the highest-paying contract in MLB history. He partied with his friends at Miami's famous South Beach to celebrate.

Stanton isn't flashy with his money, but he loves to look good. He has about 40 pairs of shoes in his closet. He enjoys combining belts and watches with fancy suits. Californians are known for their casual

style. So Stanton often wears easygoing clothes such as jeans and T-shirts.

His closets fill up quickly since he's always on the lookout for new clothes. He gathers older outfits a couple times each year. "I'll give it away to my friends or . . . people who need it," Stanton said.

## Call Me Giancarlo

Giancarlo Cruz Michael Stanton is his full name. You may know him by his nicknames Mikey or Bigfoot. His

mother refers to him as Cruz. His dad calls him Mike. "The man of a million names," Stanton joked.

Fans knew him as Mike when he joined the Marlins. He used the name because he felt it was easier to pronounce. In 2012, he asked people to begin calling him Giancarlo. But he said he'd still respond to his other names.

![Stanton and other MLB players as well as past players, such as Alex Rodriguez (right), support the Boys and Girls Clubs through MLB All-Star Week events.](image)

Stanton and other MLB players as well as past players, such as Alex Rodriguez (*right*), support the Boys and Girls Clubs through MLB All-Star Week events.

Giving away clothes is just one way that Stanton shares his time and money. In 2014, he suffered a scary injury in a game in Milwaukee, Wisconsin. A pitch struck his face, breaking bones and damaging his teeth. Stanton and the dentists who helped him heal later started All-Star Smiles. The group gives free dental care to kids. All-Star Smiles has helped hundreds of young people in the Miami area.

# JUPITER TO NEW YORK

Stanton played for the Jupiter Hammerheads in 2009.

**Stanton spent the 2007–2009 seasons in the minor leagues.** He played for teams such as the Greensboro Grasshoppers and the Jupiter Hammerheads.

Stanton played right field for
the Marlins.

He began the 2010 season in the minor leagues too.
He bashed 21 home runs in just 53 games with the
Jacksonville Suns. He was ready to play for the Marlins.

In 2010, Stanton crushed 22 home runs for the Marlins.
MLB fans were thrilled to watch the big slugger swing the
bat. His home run totals climbed. He hit 34 home runs in
2011. In 2012, he smashed 37 balls out of the park.

Stanton *(second from left)* has played with players from many other teams during All-Star Games.

The only thing slowing him down was injuries. Stanton couldn't stay on the field for a full season. He played just 116 of 162 games in 2013. Injuries to his face in 2014 kept him out for most of the 2015 season.

Stanton excelled when he was on the field. He was voted to the All-Star Game in 2012, 2014, and 2015. Finally, he put it all together in 2017. He played in 159 games, the most of his career. He led the league in home runs and played in the All-Star Game for the fourth time.

Stanton runs the bases after hitting his 58th home run in 2017.

In January 2018, Stanton attended the New York Baseball Writers' Association of America awards dinner, where he received his 2017 MVP award.

And he won the National League Most Valuable Player (MVP) award.

The season should have been reason to celebrate. Instead, Marlins players and fans dealt with big changes. The team had new owners, and they didn't want to pay all of Stanton's massive contract. They traded him to the Yankees.

Stanton was unhappy about leaving his fans in Miami. Yet he focused on the future. The Yankees are the most successful team in MLB history.

The Yankees have won the World Series 27 times. That's 16 more times than the next-best team, the St. Louis Cardinals.

Fans can expect to see many more home runs from Stanton in Yankee Stadium in the future!

Adding Stanton may be just what they need to win the World Series again. "It's going to be a great new chapter in my life," Stanton said.

# All-Star Stats

In 2017, Stanton had one of MLB's best hitting performances. How great was it? Look at this list of the most home runs in a season. It's full of famous names and legendary players.

| Player | Home Runs | Season |
| --- | --- | --- |
| Barry Bonds | 73 | 2001 |
| Mark McGwire | 70 | 1998 |
| Sammy Sosa | 66 | 1998 |
| Mark McGwire | 65 | 1999 |
| Sammy Sosa | 64 | 2001 |
| Sammy Sosa | 63 | 1999 |
| Roger Maris | 61 | 1961 |
| Babe Ruth | 60 | 1927 |
| Giancarlo Stanton | 59 | 2017 |
| Babe Ruth | 59 | 1921 |
| Ryan Howard | 58 | 2006 |
| Mark McGwire | 58 | 1997 |
| Hank Greenberg | 58 | 1938 |
| Jimmie Foxx | 58 | 1932 |
| Alex Rodriguez | 57 | 2002 |
| Luis Gonzalez | 57 | 2001 |

# Source Notes

10  Dan Martin, "Giancarlo Stanton's Surreal Rise to
    This Moment: 'He's Made for the Yankees,'" *New
    York Post*, December 12, 2017, https://nypost
    .com/2017/12/12/giancarlo-stantons-surreal-rise-to
    -this-moment-hes-made-for-the-yankees.

17  Mark Townsend, "Giancarlo Stanton Might Hit 80
    Homers Using This Wild Training Method," *Yahoo!*,
    January 20, 2018, https://sports.yahoo.com/giancarlo
    -stanton-might-hit-80-homers-using-wild-training
    -method-020219838.html.

20  Associated Press, "Marlins' Giancarlo Stanton
    Aims for a Fashion Home Run," *USA Today*, June 18,
    2016, https://www.usatoday.com/story/sports/mlb
    /2016/06/18/marlins-giancarlo-stanton-aims-for-a
    -fashion-home-run/86078322.

20  Associated Press, "Marlins RF Prefers Giancarlo
    Stanton," *ESPN*, February 29, 2012, http://www
    .espn.com/mlb/spring2012/story/_/id/7629838/spring
    -training-2012-mike-stanton-miami-marlins-wants
    -called-giancarlo-stanton.

27  Erik Boland, "Giancarlo Stanton All Smiles at First
    Yankees News Conference," *Newsday*, December 11,
    2017, https://www.newsday.com/sports/baseball
    /yankees/giancarlo-stanton-trade-official-1.15414973.

# Glossary

**batting cage:** an enclosed space for batting practice

**clinic:** an event to learn about something and gain new skills

**contract:** an agreement between an athlete and a team that determines a player's salary and time with the team

**draft:** an event in which teams take turns choosing new players

**dumbbell:** a short weighted bar used for exercise

**minor leagues:** baseball leagues where players train and hope to move up to Major League Baseball

**off-season:** the part of the year when a sports league is not playing

**pro:** something done for money that many people do for fun

**protein:** a substance in food such as eggs and fish that the body needs

**sprints:** runs at top speed for a short distance

**tee:** a post on which a ball is placed

**wide receiver:** a football player whose main job is to catch passes

**yoga:** exercises that help control the body and the mind

Fishman, Jon M. *Aaron Judge*. Minneapolis: Lerner Publications, 2019.

Giancarlo Stanton
http://m.mlb.com/player/519317/giancarlo-stanton

Kelley, K. C. *New York Yankees*. New York: AV2 by Weigl, 2018.

MLB
http://www.mlb.com/mlb/kids

Official Site of the New York Yankees
https://www.mlb.com/yankees

Savage, Jeff. *Baseball Super Stats*. Minneapolis: Lerner Publications, 2018.

# Index

# Photo Acknowledgments

Image credits: B51/Mark Brown/Getty Images Sport, p. 1; Rob Foldy/Miami Marlins/ Getty Images Sport, pp. 4–5, 6, 17, 25; Alex Trautwig/Major League Baseball/Getty Images, pp. 7, 26; ROBYN BECK/AFP/Getty Images, p. 8; Seth Poppel Yearbook Library, pp. 9, 10, 11; Rob Foldy/Getty Images Sport, p. 12; Tim Clayton-Corbis/ Corbis Sport/Getty Images, p. 13; Tom DiPace/Major League Baseball/Getty Images, p. 14; Tom Szczerbowski/Getty Images Sport, p. 15; Mike Ehrmann/Getty Images Sport, pp. 18, 23; Lester Cohen/Getty Images Entertainment, p. 19; Christian Petersen/Getty Images Sport, p. 20; Manny Hernandez/FilmMagic/Getty Images, p. 21; AP Photo/Mike Janes/FOSEAM, p. 22; Mike Ehrmann/Getty Images Sport, p. 23; Rob Carr/Getty Images Sport, p. 24.

Cover image: B51/Mark Brown/Getty Images Sport.